I0002247

Facebook Messenger Chat Bots & Marketing: The Complete Guide

SADANAND PUJARI

Published by SADANAND PUJARI, 2024.

Table of Contents

Copyright

Facebook Messenger Chat Bots & Marketing: The Complete Guide

First Edition: Jun 2024

Book Design by **SADANAND PUJARI**

About

Would you like to create chat bots for product suggestions or customer service? And have you ever thought about Facebook messenger and how to make money with it? Then this Book is for you.

In this Book, I will turn you into a professional chat bot creator & online marketer focussed on Facebook advertising. So, what are we going to learn in this Book? In the first chapter of this Book, I will show you how to create a buyer persona and launch Facebook ads. You will get a complete training Book on Facebook ads - in particular we are going to cover messages ads, and in this regard single image ads, single video ads and slideshow ads. Afterwards, we will talk about traffic and engagement ads as well as how to create cheap ads to create as much messenger traffic as possible.

In the second part of this Book, I will introduce you to Facebook chat bots and I will teach you how to create one. You will later on learn how to turn your chat bot into a customer service chat bot and products suggestions chat bot. In the last part of this Book, I will throw in my best Facebook messenger and chat bot marketing strategies for you to copy and apply.

Now, I want my students to always feel comfortable when they make a purchase, that's why I have uploaded multiple free videos for you to view at any time.

Go ahead and click the 'take this Book' button right now and I will see you in the Book. Thanks again for enrolling.

Introduction

In order to have your business succeed in the current market is imperative that you build and maintain a strong online presence with customers demanding answers at all hours of the day, regardless of what they are doing, a word they are, you should consider using a Facebook messenger, Shadbolt, that Shadbolt is an artificial intelligence, interactive messaging system that engages with your customers on behalf of your company, all using Facebook's popular messenger. And for the most part, no human is required for learning the basics of how to create one. Using a bold booting service to know what features you should have and what it should look like.

You will soon be on the way to having basic inquiries on products and services to sales, sometimes within minutes. Gone are the days of people only being able to call customer service Monday through Friday and to 5:00 p.m.. Not only do they want answers to their questions right away, but they no longer have to leave their home in order to make a purchase. An interactive chat board is a perfect tool for any online business. Technology is here to stay, and the customers love how A saves them so much time. Chatterbox with severe post time and money since it takes away the costs of traditional person failed labor positions. So if you like more information on how to successfully build one, keep watching this Book.

Customer FAQs

When creating a chat about your Facebook Messenger marketing campaign, you may feel overwhelmed at what you should and should not include in May. After all, you don't want to inundate your customer with so much information that they lose interest in your product, which is why you should refer to your company's most frequent questions. Have been accused. Consider sending out a broadcast email or hosting a Facebook live chapter and see what questions are doing your event. You can discuss your product during the event or even just use it as a basic get to know us interaction with your audience. Pay attention to the questions that keep popping off the most.

For example, do you offer free shipping on large orders for exchanges and return promotions when you go to Pujari Facebook Messenger Chapel, including these F.A.A.? Q So the customer can easily interact with them? Within the past month, my current and potential new customers are learning more about your business through a chat board that is being crafted with their own personal touch. Customers don't want to hear a basic yes or no, even though they know they are talking with a shadbolt, they still want that human touch. For more tips on how to personalize your tablet for your own business. Check out this article from Intrapreneur that gives some great tips and tricks to keeping your customer engaged and also attached the link.

Automated Greeting

Up to you deciding on what customer FNQ to add to your Facebook Messenger tablet, you should consider adding a warm and inviting automated greeting. A potential customer is browsing your Facebook page, taking a look at a customer's comments and your posts and deciding to reach out to our chapel where you might think a basic hello is good enough. The truth is that customers don't want Gudina. They want to be woad. And with so many companies Algier nowadays, it's imperative that you make your stand up. So think outside of the box and then refrain from something generic. Consider a greeting that is to be more welcoming, welcoming such as greetings, welcome to such as a company and what brings you here today.

Remember that when you are in a sales environment it's important to ask open ended questions saying something like, Are you having a good day? Can we interest you in such a product? Will it result in a bailout or a negative response? Encourage a customer to have an engaging conversation with our chapel while the customer is interacting with their Chabert overmodulated choice answers that gradually narrow down to very specific questions tailored to their needs. A simple interest in your body lotion. But the price is a little too high for me to lead to a sale. Or is there something else your offer or discount if they get it with another product? Just remember to keep your customer engaged in a casual conversation. Don't be too pushy and don't sound robotic, too warm and inviting.

Make it seem as though they are really talking with a human and Of course allows them to ask the child at any time. Customers never want to feel obligated into doing something they don't want to. There are lots of successful Chappells Aldar for you to look at and we encourage you to do so. You can get an idea of how you want to look as well. Pay attention to the ones that are the most successful and about how a similar one would work well for your own business. For an idea of what a successful Chappells looks like, as well as other tips for making your just as successful Checo marketing 360 Balcon is full of information. You can put it to good use with your own Chappellet.

Casual Conversation Vs. Shop Button

If you ever visit our Facebook page, then you might have been shocked by the Army is pretty self-explanatory. Customers can simply click on that button. It takes them to an e-commerce store. But customers don't need to engage with a shadbolt in order to hit that bottle. So should you bother putting one into your tablet? It's a good idea to have a shot button, but you want to encourage your customers to either act with your shadbolt rather than just hitting that bottom, especially since interacting with a tablet has a better chance of having them spend more money, whereas just hitting the shot button will result in them by what they are looking for. And not one sure tablet recommends based on their conversation. First of all, remember that casual conversation is almost always a little more selfs.

That's the more your chapel talks, the more it relaxes the customer and makes them feel at ease when they are feeling at ease that they are less likely to say no to products your Chappells suggests. But that doesn't mean you shouldn't have a Schobert in at some point during a conversation between your Chabert and the customer. So will probably be interested enough to buy something your Chabert can be programmed to insert links to products. Or you can have a simple shot button within the chapel. Better yet, you have both. This gives the customer the option to continue chatting or leaving the chapel or shop on their own. Just remember that most customers are more likely to give up business their hard earned money if it offers direct, 24/7 friendly customer service. So keep the conversation friendly and your Charbel available as open as possible.

Finding Your Audience

If you're watching this Book, the chances are good you have an inking, your audience have some presence on Facebook, but before you consider building a chapel just for their messengers platform, you should verify that it is worth their time and money. Consider sending an email to customers who are on your mailing list and ask them to tell you where they spend a lot of their social media time not to be too invasive about your personal lives, but also enough to know how often the platform has over a billion users worldwide. It's safe to say that most people use Facebook and their messenger application, and studies show that customers are more likely to open their application.

Instead, on email from a company, a symbol feels more personal, almost as though they are chatting with a friend or family member, even though they are talking about buying something from a business troubled. Even if you decide not to view the table for their messenger platform, you should still rarely find a Facebook page for your business. If enough of your customers use a messenger application, then you should be who you are to build a chapel. Be sure to add a chapel to your Facebook page for customers to see eye to eye and remember that customers can see your response rate right on your Facebook page at the top below your business name.

Be like with your taxes within the chapel customer. Don't respond well to a lot of verbiage. They want a friendly response, but not a bunch of the words they have to wade through.

Remember that we will have a conversation not sitting down to read and to reply to some mass email from a business. It's a good idea to leave about three seconds before sending a message, sending a message back to back. We'll make a customer feel rushed, which won't leave them with a good impression of your company at any point during our table conversation. Remember to give users the option to unsubscribe and as if the Chabert.

Promoting Your Chatbot

What is the point of creating a Facebook messenger tablet if a customer doesn't know that it is available, you shall make a point to promote the new program across several social media platforms if you want to build and maintain a successful business. You have to engage current and potential customers and customers want immediate results, letting them know why our Facebook advertisement and other forums online that have an interactive chappellet is a great way to catch their attention. Consider taking a Facebook advertisement where your customer tends to shop. For example, if your business is selling sunglasses, then create ads that will appear on Facebook pages related to our shopping.

People will see how to or to your page and have the option to engage with your Chabert advertising. Your table is just as important as advertising anything else for your business as he has the potential to bring a lot of revenue. There are still customers out there who think they have to wait on hold for a representative when in reality they can get an answer within a few seconds when it comes to creating their travel. There are many options out there for you. A few examples of the travel tools that you can use at screen chat and chat, a few and mobile money.

Educate Customers

Once customers fund, would you have a chapel, do you all want to take a moment and ask them about all the features? For example, it's a good idea to give your child a name that is unique to your business. If your company is selling floral arrangements, then come up with something interesting that incorporates the flowers and seems friendly to the customers. Tell your customers that was the purpose of your trip. Is it to answer questions, suggest products or just for general common customers? Want to know why you are creating this travel and why they should take the time to use it. You will also want to let the customer know that the saleability of your travel, even though it is EHI, is still on a human level in case something goes wrong with it.

It's a technology. If something goes wrong, word therapy, someone right away to fix it or they have to weigh customers have made it clear that they want transparency when dealing with a business. They want to know what they are dealing with and who is getting their money. Make it clear that your chapel is there to make the shopping experience easier and that if anything could be wrong, a human will be there with them shortly. And to finally tell the customer what a possibility is that these scrambled can do everything from start to finish work on its face. A product in your home so you can see if you like it. Customers Wilsonville before they give you their business.

Security

Ferbos can retain a lot of information about your customers, just think of the last time you look at the product on the website and saw an ad for it on social media, just like a cookie sourced information, Soldo Chappells and a customer want to know that their information is as safe as they can be in my added expense. But nowadays you really need to invest in security, like creating your tablet.

After all, it has the potential to remember everything from what you would send your mom for her birthday to your credit card information? Reassure your customers that you can be trusted.

Design A Chatbot Character

In my song, City, buzzing about designing a word of character for your child, just like a guy has a gecko, your cable, she has something funny and interesting to keep customers engaged and if possible, keep it related to your business. For example, if your business is selling Paquita Goose, then perhaps your travel should be a cartoon bigger. Or if you are a massive online retailer with the sales as a product of truth from maybe just a witty shopping cart, you can talk. Everyone likes to have fun. And even adults who have a kick out of a car trunk toppled, interacting with them about a product you've come to offer, especially since so many of us fund the shopping. A relaxing, enjoyable hobby wouldn't be a funny cartoon.

Make it even better. One that can answer your questions and why we are on the topic is being funny. Don't hesitate to throw some emojis and funny gifs. Customers love to have a good time while they are shopping. Just keep in mind that different people have different types of humor, so keep it as family friendly as possible. For example, if your child will realize that the customer will love a certain product code, it is a sort of funny gift or some smiling or grabbing their purse. Just make sure that it's interactive and encourage them to have fun and most importantly, buy that product.

Combine with Facebook Live

Getting back to collecting customer FNQ, consider having a Facebook chapter and having your child interact with customers in the comments is a great way to engage them and then respond in real time as their table is made. You are in your Facebook alive chapter utilizing a customer will see that it is so personal so it can actually respond to pretty specific questions. For example, if you ask a customer what their budget is and they give a number, they automatically show them a product within that price range. This is also a great time for returning customers to interact with a chapel and for new customers to see how he remembers information which allows for easy upselling and more money for your business.

You can also lose a face to a laugh chapter for the launch of a new product. Will your new child, at the very same time use that time to educate customers on the tablet? Why they should use it at the same time, get to know your customers. Give them the option to interact directly with a Chabert so they can see how it works. Most people will love how personal a channel can be and appreciate that it saves them time. And Of course, before talking about your new product.

Include Send Message In

Anyone who has ever used Facebook has seen an advertisement for a new product with white movie or product. As previously mentioned, we often find ourselves online shopping sites before heading over to Facebook and Walia. An advertisement for that very same product appears in our feed. This is a great opportunity to incorporate a send a message button within a Facebook ad. Customers will see an ad for your business describing what services you offer and have the option just to click, send a message.

It's another way to streamline someone who stumbles upon your ad like what they see and then makes a purchase all within a matter of minutes. This is why it is important that you make sure that you are buying Facebook ads for your business too, and making sure that they pop up when customers are likely to see them. If you never take our Facebook ad, there are tutorials and books out there that can show you how adding a send the message is very easy. Anyone who shops online and uses Facebook knows how easy it is to buy something. So why not make it even either?

Conclusion

When creating your chapel to just remember, to keep things in mind, first and foremost, the goal of the chapel is to save time for customers shopping. It's faster and easier than ever before. Your customers are still looking for ways to streamline the process. Studies show that it's best to keep the point of sale under five clicks, address any concerns they have as some open ended question, and then direct them to whatever it is they are looking for. Anything more will often result in losing a sale. Be transparent with your customer at all times and be sure to include an option to end the conversation at any time. There's no point in keeping someone engaged who isn't going to buy anything. Have fun when creating your tablet and good luck in the girls and the future of your business.

Case Studies

Congratulations on finishing this Book. However, this is only the beginning, not the end. The next stop, you will have to apply what you have learned in this Book to the real world. You might feel a little scared initially, ready to dive into the real business world all along. But do not worry about that. I'm here for you. The next chapter of this Book is a continuation series of weekly business case studies. So every week I will send you one new educational video of a real world business case study.

In this study, I will show you exactly how I came out with this business idea. It could be entrepreneurship or it could be investing. Right. And step by step, details on how I put them into practice. And finally, I will show you the real world result, what kind of business revenue will be achieved, what kind of business we made so that you don't have to repeat it right. And you can learn from that and understand how this business idea works. So stay tuned to our weekly case study.

And if you have any questions, I will go online to do a live QA to explain to you and interact with you to help you succeed in your business and in your investing projects. I'm hearing down here, I sincerely hope you like this Book and also join us in the weekly case study. I will be connecting you through your journey of this learning and starting your own business, and I hope you become successful in every aspect of your life. So thank you so much for taking this Book. I will see you in the next weekly case studies.

Bonus

Hello and congratulations on finishing out your Facebook messenger, Of course, in this bonus chapter, and I want to share with you my first hand experience, how I leveraged his Facebook messenger into your online marketing campaign to help you attract to higher conversion rate and also getting more traffic and more satisfaction for your customers. As you can see on my background, this is my official Website for my own blog. Right. I was actually highlighting a series of product pronouncers I'm offering right now.

I want to teach people how to access Stahler's successful trading business. A lot of people here use the Internet either to have a YouTube channel or to have their own blog to teach people how to make money online or about making money allies to join or racing to do. And a lot of people will talk about how they can start drop shopping or to our e-commerce business or other people. What teaches them how to print a book is a kind of self publishing business, like creating a YouTube channel. Right. For me, my background in the society of trading, by growing at all, we're all at a cost. Stock futures, forex and also cryptocurrency. Right.

And I'm using the systematic trading method. That means how all the different fruiting style or that fruiting organisms strategy pre-programmed or their everyday, they just automatically download and run the program to give you the insight about what is going to happen tomorrow for the financial market, give us a prediction based on machine learning models or based also systematic rules you've already found, but also food that has to show you that Holley's other strategy, worthwhile or bad in the past, that you can decide what kind of strategy you want to replicate in the future.

Not necessarily. You can replicate 100 percent of the strategy, but it's a good starting point to sink and work in a systematic way instead of having to run the fitting that I have on the trail at this trial. That's not right. That's not a long term way to approach Fredi. I want to teach people how I can. You can actually start treating business, not treating, treating, treating as some kind of hobby or just dabbling. No, you don't want to do that. You want to start a serious business. Consider what is a budget for your business, housesitter. What is Cantus's revenue projection or what is a product you want to get to the market and what to do if the idea about this market is good or not? Right.

All those years I was sitting in my plop rack, but you see, I have my block there and I have to bring bartender invite people to actually check out my free Trinian's Fatsos personalized product. You don't want to get people to buy it instantly because it's not like e-commerce products, physical products, small items, household items that people aren't familiar with is right, even though they actually do not know your product, but they probably have tried some different products before somewhere else. Someone else. That's right. Before those highly customizable and a business product, people want to give them individual rights. They want to come back to your block several times. Right.

They want to check out everything. They probably want to review what is your free training and what is your self introduction and what you can do in your own block. Right. And what is offered for you or other resources that you crave that have operators. Right. And a topic that people really want to come back to. Please do. You can click the green button to actually connect with you by watching your free training videos. Right. And then you can follow up with some emails and keep in touch. Otherwise, because Facebook and Social Network is so popular right now, everybody has a Facebook or Instagram user.

Wamsley's right. Because you really want to engage people with Facebook messages. And then when you actually click the Facebook manager, what you see, you want to see that? Do you want to interact with them? Right. You can select your role. Depends on your privacy settings. You can decide to use Ghast or use your own name. And when you click in there, right, the physical messenger will actually start to greet you. Right. It's all about customer service experience. I guess, when you are your customer. To visit a Web site and teachers see a blank Web page.

Sir, you have a lot of content. There are a lot of videos or a lot of options there for them to choose from. Right. But if you do not install a Facebook messenger, there will be one thing missing from the page of what they are already familiar with. Right. Because everybody is on Facebook. And when you are shown that Facebook messenger that everybody knows what it is and they automatically know that you are offering some customer service request and they are so accessible, everyone cliqued up on it, then that started chatting with you. Right. And that you can even set out to Automatic Imadi to actually give the service automates. Right.

Automotive service for the common questions. For the comments. Questions to answer. You just give it all the least, a common question of values, or there's another service that you can ask the customers or get in touch with. Either calling your phone number or sending some emails to you is your choice. You have so much flexibility to do this, right? You can do the same thing here in your application. So, you know, plop itself right. You can spend this in this Facebook messenger that gives you the flexibility that is an independent component. You can replicate this same coupling at the same place to a manager, a messenger, to every single application in your piece or another website.

You can apply the same way, but you are collecting the same message to you as a product developer of this whole block or an application you are promoting. Right. You are really connected with people in the same way as a fiscal manager as the traditional email that it can be offline to. Right. Even though you might not be online when people are reaching out to you to ask for help. Right. But you can start to see the message whenever you are online again, and from there you can start to actually connect with people. And another good, strong benefit is because everybody is on Facebook. Right.

And if you think you have those messages for your customers, when you actually see the message, you can actually see who they are. Right. From the Facebook profile. Right. You can check out their profile to see what is their life update or how they are feeling about their life and what kind of really serious problems they have in their life that they need your help to achieve. These are some they're starting off a new business or they're considering to test the water in the trading business. Right. Those are the things that you can try and you can engage them with. Right. Because everybody is on Facebook. And also if you have a selected Facebook pixel. Right.

Web sites and whenever and in one company, you sort of Facebook manager, they will automatically be reported into the Facebook message pixel. Right. So the pixel will know whoever clicks on your page or interacts with or interacts with your physical messenger. And they don't check back to the Facebook database to see who they are and who actually they can retaliate. Right. That means that if you have one customer leaving a message that they can make the purchase decisions right away. Right. Buzz through the Facebook pixel. You can try to check more details, who they are, what is the status of their business and that you can consider to target them.

That means that you can send some follower emails or text messages before they leave your phone numbers and you can actually connect with them and offer something different. Maybe the all right price you are offering is not the ideal price they want to have. Right. But you definitely can give them something different. And to get them back to your website, get them back to consider buying your products for one of them. Right. So those are the strong benefits of Facebook Messenger. If you are using email, you don't have to have a benefit because the email, even though Pixel will record it right.

Whoever clicks on your Web site sort of cookie or through the sort of email address, maybe you said leave your email address, but you never get a full picture of the customer information like Facebook or Facebook, Amazon visiting you. It's just one person. Right, and the other side of the email or cookie. Only guessing, right, whoever it is might be right or not right. But Facebook Messenger is so powerful to have the social media power injected into your Web site right away. Right. And literally turn your own blog into another social media site where I think people automatically lock in with their social media profile. Right. This could never happen.

Any other blog, if you don't install, are able to feature a social event, right? I mean, you allow people to lobby using a Facebook account to our. Right. But if you do not want to introduce complicated authentication features into your passport application, you can simply check this Facebook messenger. Right. Because when our people click on those messengers to chat with you, they're automatically looking at the Facebook account. And, you know, it's always good to talk to you and tell them what kind of help they need from you. Right. Those are strong benefits to this. Right.

And also, whenever you define your customer service manuals, I. I suggest to you to sing about the full picture of those things that you want to offer right now just to introduce your product, which is very important as well for mature, and helped him to explain the details of what your product is and what you what kind of problem you are trying to sow and whatever other situations. Right. And the thing that you want to really get to know your customers, you can use your Facebook messenger, you can set out a whole list of questions to ask your customers, whatever. Right. Gives them the option to choose A or right to understand their situations in detail.

So you can set up questions like what is your what is our business status? Is it newly created or are you considering starting your own business? Or are your experiences with the business owners who want to try trading this afternoon that you can understand? What is your experience with treating yourself right and what kind of market you have been training for, what kind of strategy you have been trading for? And what is it? Because they are treating and if you're treating so well, then what? We can help you to actually get your training to the next level.

All right. If you're not truly successful in the past, then what kind of service or product are you actually looking for from us? We can help you. And also the questions are the questions to get people up to speed and get them to know that you are actually helping them. All right. You are really small, like a consulting role that you get people to get people to. You are offering their help to your customer for free. And it's very customizable. That means you do not offer a standard product right from the beginning. Instead, you work with each of the customers to understand their situation through the Facebook messenger. It's like a survey, right, to ask you to ask your customers.

And then from there you can run there. You can ask them to. From there, you can ask them to. I tried to see what the service is to help you want them to get it. So it's highly customizable and it really helps you to understand your customer better. And if you are not a customer or potential customer better, you definitely can't get them to the two words and into your long term customers or their loyal customers. Right. Because you really know them. You really want to help them. And that's our biggest advantage, compared to other service providers who simply want to take their offer, take their order and, you know, just want to make some short term money. No, you don't want to do that.

You want to engage them in the long term. And that's the right way to actually actually help you to actually become more successful with your business development. Right. Always, always, always engage your customers in different channels in different ways. These are social network izabella email or this chapter, like the social media messengers are always Chavism. Keep the communication flowing. Right. And if you're chatting through the Facebook messenger to like a 1000 people and you have so much information, valuable information to actually come back to create your product, make your product better.

So those are credible information that you should definitely, definitely do if you can get to that. Right. I hope you learn a lot from this Book. And I hope you can leverage the power of the Facebook messenger into your own website or sorest to help you to actually understand your customer better and actually getting more information as to how to improve the coverage and traffic site on your online business. And I want to see you on my next call. Thank you.